First published in 1993
© The Estate of Jane Miller 1993
All rights reserved

A VANESSA HAMILTON BOOK
produced in association with
N T Productions, Copenhagen

Photographic research: Malvin van Gelderen
Book design: Jesper Søholm

ISBN 0 7500 1305 2

Simon & Schuster Young Books
Campus 400
Maylands Avenue
Hemel Hempstead
Herts HP2 7EZ

Printed by N T Productions in Malaysia

In the same series
COLOURS ON THE FARM

BABY
ANIMALS
ON
THE FARM

Jane Miller

SIMON & SCHUSTER
YOUNG BOOKS

A baby cow is a **calf**.

This Jersey calf is only a few hours old.

He is carefully looked after by his mother. When she has licked him clean, the calf will drink from her udder.

A baby cat is a **kitten**.

Kittens are lively and curious.
They love exploring the farm.

The barn is a
favourite place to
play . . .

and the trailer's
mudguard makes
a good seat in
the sun.

A baby goose is a **gosling**.

Goslings are covered with yellow down
when they are young.

This Canada goose is starting to teach her young to swim.

A baby donkey is a **foal**.

The young donkey suckles milk from his mother.

A baby pig is a **piglet**.

The mother pig, or sow, usually gives birth to at least six piglets at a time, sometimes more.

How many can you count in these pictures?

A baby duck is a **duckling**.

A mallard duck's young are brown and yellow. As soon as they can, the ducklings take to the water.

A baby dog is a **puppy**.

This mother collie has six puppies to feed.

The farmer is about to give these puppies milk from a bottle.

A baby sheep is a **lamb**.

A ewe, or mother sheep, often gives birth to twin lambs — either outside (where their fleecy coats protect them from cold winds), or inside a warm barn.

A baby hen is a **chick**.

A Bantam
chick nestles
in its mother's
feathers to
keep warm.
Chicks learn
to scratch for
worms and
insects in the
farmyard.

A baby swan is a **cygnet**.

Cygnets are covered in soft grey down. When they start to swim, they take care to stay close to their mother.

A baby horse is a **foal**.

A foal can stand on its long, wobbly legs just a few minutes after being born.

A foal drinks milk from its mother, but also crops grass soon after it is born.

A baby goat is a **kid**.

This nanny goat is the mother of twins. Goats can eat almost anything, but the kids' first food is milk.

Can you name the baby animals
in these four pictures?

It is always fun
to play with
baby animals on
a farm!